Deinosuchus

Written by David White
Illustrated by Pam Mara

LIBRARY OF CONGRESS
Library of Congress
Cataloging-in-Publication Data

White, David, 1952 July 13–
    Deinosuchus / by David White;
    illustrated by Pam Mara.
        p.   cm — (Dinosaur library)
        Summary: Describes a day in the life of the large,
    cold-blooded dinosaur known as Deinosuchus with
    information about his physical characteristics, habits,
    and natural environment.
        ISBN 0-86592-524-0
        1. Deinosuchus—Juvenile literature.
    [1. Deinosuchus. 2. Dinosaurs.] I. Mara, Pamela, ill.
    II. Title. III. Series.
    QE862.C8W49 1988
    567.9'7—dc 19   88-5973
                                                            CIP
                                                            AC

Rourke Enterprises, Inc.
Vero Beach, FL 32964

Quetzalcoatlus

Parasaurolphus

Deinosuchus

Corythasaurus

Spinosaurus

Oviraptor

Deinosuchus

Pachycephalosaurus

Anatosaurus

Struthiomimus

Scolosaurus

Rutiodon

Psittacosaurus

It was still dark as Deinosuchus glided slowly through the river. He swam silently, his enormous bulk causing scarcely a ripple on the still water. Only the tip of his large snout and his small but ever watchful eyes could be seen above the surface.

Dawn was near. Growing light began to reveal the features of the riverside: muddy inlets, tall grasses and trees whose exposed roots seemed to writhe like snakes.

Deinosuchus had been active all night, snapping up fish and other small land creatures that had crossed his path. Now he was filled. In spite of his great size, he needed little food to sustain his life.

Deinosuchus needed to warm his blood. He swam toward the inlet that marked the boundary of his territory. With a mighty rush of water he surfaced. Plegadornis, hunting in the shallow waters of the inlet for frogs and water beetles, flew off in alarm. Lizards, alerted by the vast shadow of Deinosuchus, scurried into the long grass.

Deinosuchus drew his great length up the bank and lumbered toward the glade where he usually basked with his mate. Suddenly, he heard a long drawn out hiss. A few yards away, and across his path, stood another huge crocodilian. He was a rival of Deinosuchus, always ready to fight for the position of leader of the pack.

Deinosuchus did not hesitate. With a roar, he launched himself at his adversary. The riverbank seemed to shake with the shock of the impact. The two creatures twisted and turned, thrashing their huge tails. Each of them was trying to knock the other off balance. This would expose the throat and belly, the only areas of the heavily armored creatures which were vulnerable to attack.

The struggle was soon over, for this was no fight to the death, but a trial of strength. Deinosuchus was clearly the stronger of the two. His rival accepted this and backed away. Hissing discontentedly, he slunk into the long grass and disappeared from view.

His dominance confirmed, Deinosuchus continued on his way. Soon he found the spot where his mate and other crocodilians were basking motionless in the sun. Deinosuchus settled his massive body on the grass and let the sun warm the cold blood in his veins.

By now the sun was rising in a clear blue sky. Butterflies and bees moved among the climbing roses and banks of saxifrage which surrounded the glade. As Deinosuchus basked, smaller creatures scampered by at a respectful distance. Struthiomimus appeared, plucking fruit and leaves from the trees with her long arms. Her appetite seemed insatiable, as she plucked insects from the air with her horny beak and grabbed at lizards in the long grass.

Deinosuchus remained watchful. Such creatures were
poor prey, since they could easily outrun him. However, some
of them could be a real threat. Velociraptor, in particular,
had a taste for crocodilian eggs. Fortunately, the female
crocodilians buried their nests very deep in the sand. By the
time Velociraptor had discovered the eggs, Deinosuchus had
usually discovered him. Velociraptor never stayed to argue,
but darted off with astonishing speed.

When the sun had reached its highest point, and day was at its hottest, Deinosuchus stirred. By now his blood was warm. He felt active and alert. He raised his body from the ground and waddled across the glade. Now it was time to hunt in the cool shade of the forest pools.

A herd of Parasaurolophus were browsing on the upper branches of the pines at the forest's edge. Their teeth ground the tough needles to a green pulp. As Deinosuchus approached they moved away quickly, back to the trees which they had already stripped bare of foliage.

Deinosuchus entered the forest pool with surprising quietness. Even so the sound was enough to alert Alamosaurus, wading in the pool a hundred yards away. Alamosaurus slowly turned his head and gazed at Deinosuchus. Cautiously, he began to lumber away. Deinosuchus did not bother to follow, but slid down into the water, half in and half out, like a giant trunk of some fallen oak. Nearby, a python uncurled itself from a branch and disappeared into the ferns.

Deinosuchus had picked a good position. He was completely hidden by the shade of the forest. The sunlight which filtered through the pines and cypresses served only to camouflage him further. At the same time, he had a good view of the pool and of any creature who came to drink at it.

He did not have to wait long. A herd of
Corythosaurus moved slowly down to the waterside. Yards
from the pool, they stopped. Their keen sense of smell and
hearing warned them of danger. They could sense
Deinosuchus, although they could not see him.

One Corythosaurus, younger and more impatient
than the rest, walked down to the water and began to drink,
only inches from where Deinosuchus lay.

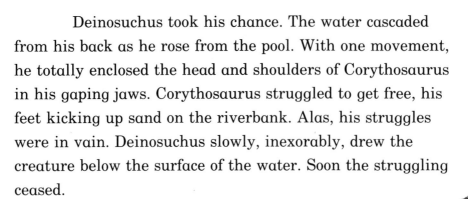

Deinosuchus took his chance. The water cascaded from his back as he rose from the pool. With one movement, he totally enclosed the head and shoulders of Corythosaurus in his gaping jaws. Corythosaurus struggled to get free, his feet kicking up sand on the riverbank. Alas, his struggles were in vain. Deinosuchus slowly, inexorably, drew the creature below the surface of the water. Soon the struggling ceased.

Deinosuchus was preparing to drag the dead
Corythosaurus to his larder below the branches of a giant
sequoia, when he heard a roar. The herd of Corythosaurus
had vanished. In their place stood the towering figure of
Tyrannosaurus.

Deinosuchus feared no creature, however large. He
angrily turned to face Tyrannosaurus putting himself
between him and the carcass of Corythosaurus.

Tyrannosaurus lurched forward, lunging at Deinosuchus in an effort to frighten him. Deinosuchus held his ground. Tyrannosaurus tried to snatch at the carcass. Deinosuchus lashed his tail fiercely, almost knocking Tyrannosaurus off balance.

Soon Tyrannosaurus grew tired. He wanted food not a fight. Eventually, he stalked away, leaving Deinosuchus with his prey. As Tyrannosaurus left, his body cast a giant shadow on the grass. The day was drawing to a close.

The reconstructed skeleton of Deinosuchus compared in size with a man.

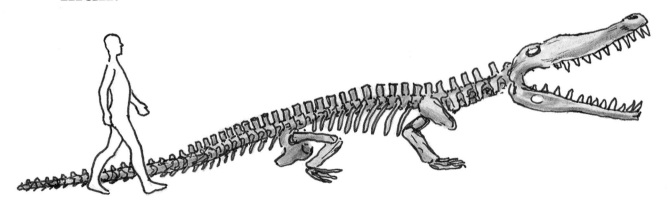

Length: Only a 6 ft (1.8 m) skull has been discovered. This would give Deinosuchus a probable length of 40–50 ft (12–15 m).

Deinosuchus and Late Cretaceous Texas

The time of Deinosuchus

Scientists divide the Earth's history over the last 600 million years into three eras – the Paleaozoic, Mesozoic and Cenozoic. They subdivide these eras into periods. The Mesozoic ("middle era"), known as the Age of the Dinosaurs, had three periods – the Triassic, Jurassic and Cretaceous. The Triassic period lasted from 225 to 195 million years ago, the Jurassic from 195 to 136 million years ago, and the Cretaceous – the longest period of all – from 136 to 65 million years ago. The Cretaceous period was the time of Deinosuchus.

The land of Deinosuchus

The fossilized remains of Deinosuchus have been found in the rock formations of the Rio Grande, Texas. The area is rich in dinosaur remains. Indeed, the entire range of known dinosaur orders and suborders of the Late Cretaceous period have been discovered in locations in western North America and Alberta, Canada. The land was changing fast at that time. The seas had flooded Europe and receded from North America, leaving behind inland seas and areas of swamp. Flora and fauna which are familiar to us today were evolving. Trees like magnolia, plane and oak, flowering plants, moths, butterflies and pollinating bees, all began to appear. Giant sequoias and swamp cypresses grew in the swampy area where this story is set.

Family tree of Deinosuchus

Like dinosaurs, crocodiles evolved from the thecodont ("socket toothed") reptiles more than 200 million years ago. The first crocodilian was Protosuchus, whose remains were discovered in Arizona. This small, bony plated, amphibious reptile lived in the Upper (or later) Triassic period. In the Upper Jurassic and Lower Cretaceous a number of sea crocodiles known as mesosuchians evolved. Earliest of these was Pelagosaurus, which fed mainly on fish. Sea crocodiles differed in many ways from land crocodiles. They had no armor plating and they had flippers instead of limbs. Mesosuchians were followed by land based sebecosuchians, and amphibious eusuchians – the only kind of crocodile that survives today. Deinosuchus was a eusuchian.

Other meat eaters

Many kinds of carnivorous (meat eating) dinosaurs lived at the time of Deinosuchus. Perhaps the most impressive was Tyrannosaurus, the largest bi-ped (two-footed) ever to walk the earth. Although we know what Tyrannosaurus and the other carnosaurs looked like, we do not know how they lived. The traditional view is that these creatures were cold-blooded. If so, they would not have had the energy to pursue their prey. Instead they would have relied on ambush, or scavenged the remains of other animals' kills. However, some scientists now believe flesh eaters were warm blooded. If this was so, they may have hunted their prey, singly or in packs, over long distances. Coelurosaurs such as Struthiomimus and Velociraptor are always counted as flesh eating dinosaurs but actually they were descendants of flesh eaters who had become mainly vegetarian. They should perhaps be described as omnivorous, because they ate anything they could find — including dinosaur eggs.

Plant eaters

Herbivores (plant-eating animals) far outnumbered carnivores in this period. There were still a few giant sauropods, such Alamosaurus (named after the Alamo in Texas). However most of the famous sauropods, such as Diplodocus had died out million of years before. Their place was taken by ornithopods, notably the hadrosaurs, such as the helmeted Corythosaurus and the tube crested Parasaurolophus. (Nobody knows the purpose of these crests. They may have been recognition signals). These creatures, which are also known as duck billed dinosaurs, were immensely successful, spreading from Asia to Europe and North America. The secret of their success may have been their teeth, which could grind down the toughest foliage for food. Had the carnosaurs not kept their numbers down, they would have browsed the forests bare.

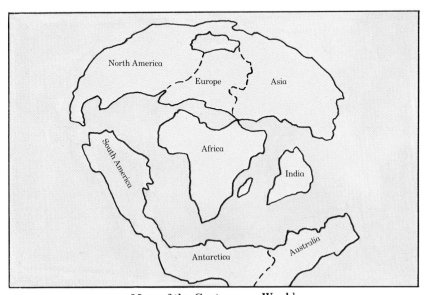

Map of the Cretaceous World